D1269653

finding His strength

An Orphan's Journey to Healing and Wholeness

Estelle H. Herndon

Finding His Strength
© Copyright 2016 Estelle H. Herndon

ISBN-13: 978-1-944120-21-4
ISBN-10: 1-944120-21-1
E-book ISBN-13: 978-1-944120-22-1
Large Print: 978-1-944120-25-2

Published by TMP Books, 2631 Holly Springs Pkwy. Box 35,
Holly Springs, GA 30142

www.TMPBooks.com

Published in the United States of America.

finding His strength

An Orphan's Journey to Healing and Wholeness

Estelle H. Herndon

Finding His Strength
© Copyright 2016 Estelle H. Herndon

ISBN-13: 978-1-944120-21-4
ISBN-10: 1-944120-21-1
E-book ISBN-13: 978-1-944120-22-1
Large Print: 978-1-944120-25-2

Published by TMP Books, 2631 Holly Springs Pkwy. Box 35,
Holly Springs, GA 30142

www.TMPBooks.com

Published in the United States of America.

Dedication

The fern on the cover is dedicated
to my mother, Avey.
The rocks represent how hard early life was
for my brother and me.

Dedication

To Robert, my wonderful husband.
He is my joy, my love, always reminding me what a
"Good God" we serve. He is solid, practical, a giver
not a taker in life. He keeps me anchored, always
reminding me to look up, not down.

I love him saying "I'm his best friend." His wisdom
blows me away. There is nothing he wouldn't do for
me. Thank you, Lord. A Gift from God no doubt.

CONTENTS

A Personal Letter to My Readers

Traveling through life is not an easy task, especially when abuse, whether physical, sexual, or verbal, is a main factor.

I write this letter to serve as a source of encouragement for you, the reader.

Without our Lord, we cannot make it. From Psalm 91, I have learned in my personal walk that HE is my shelter, I'm safe in HIS hiding place. HE strengthens my faith, calms my fears and HE can do the same for you if you just let HIM. Ask HIM to come into your heart and heal all your broken places, like He's done for me.

He guards each and every step we make, protects us because HE knows our names, answers prayers, even if it's not the answer we requested. HE sees the big picture, we don't.

Stay in HIS word, my friends (The BOOK of Life — the Bible), pray without ceasing, in good times and bad, honor HIM always even though the difficulties in your life.

HE cares, and so do I. Rest in HIS arms. Sleeplessness in the face of our everyday circumstances could be a sure sign our focus is in the wrong place. Remember, our Problem Solver never sleeps.

Leave yesterday behind, His mercies are new every day. He used the ugly in my life to bring support to you, my friends.

He saved me and I pray He'll do the same for you. Heaven awaits those who truly believe and follow Him.

Romans 8:28 is so true in my life because God works through all things for the good of all His children.

Introduction

My entering this world must have been hard on my family. I think I was born at home where the doctor came when the baby was due, then left without putting a name on my birth certificate. I only had "female" on my birth certificate, no name, just "female." This is how my life started and the documentation stayed that way until I was sixty-three and applied for early social security. Social Security would not accept my birth certificate.

As a child, I had been called "Estelle," so I named myself "Vera Estelle Haralson." After my attorney insisted I had to have two names, I was sitting at my desk when the name "Vera" came to mind. That's how I became Vera Estelle Haralson. Praise the Lord a birth certificate wasn't required in applying for a job or attending school, for that matter.

I'm the only person I know of who named herself. This shock wave introduced me into "not belonging to anyone." Later, after accepting Jesus, I realized that I am somebody – a child of King Jesus. He knows my name. I am His and He is mine. Never will I forget this.

I am now the young age of 75. Young at heart, but if you look close enough at my face, those wrinkles tell a different story. Fifty years ago, God blessed me with a handsome husband, cute as can be. I also work with him. I have a great son, sweet daughter-in-law, beautiful daughter, wonderful niece and her caring husband, sweet granddaughter, three awesome grandsons and one great-grandson. What a delight they are to me. I'm known as "Momma," "Mom," "Essie," "Nana," names that melt my heart away. They are sweet, sweet jewels from my Lord!

Other names I am known by include "Cupcake," "Gardelia," and "S."

I have held back on revealing my life story as it has been very painful. God, through the Holy Spirit, used a Bible study teacher to nudge me along in sharing just how our Lord had worked in my life and carried me in HIS strength as HE does today. She told her story and how she started writing, encouraging all of us to do the same.

My prayer is that in some way my journey through life's struggles will draw you closer to HIM. If you don't know HIM, pray and ask HIM to come into your heart, forgive you of your sins and take Him as your Savior. That is all it takes. What an awesome peace this will bring to you. One more thing, you must, and I say this again MUST, forgive yourself, for HE has plans for you, just as HE had for me. Plans to prosper you, not to cause you any harm.

FEAR

"When I am afraid, I put my trust in you. In God, whose word I praise—in God I trust and am not afraid. What can mere mortals do to me?"
Psalm 56:3-4 NIV

"What, then shall we say in response to this? If God be for us, who can be against us?"
Romans 8:31 NIV

"So do not fear, for I am with you; do not be dismayed, for I am your God. I will strengthen you and help you; I will uphold you with my righteous right hand."
Isaiah 41:10 NIV

FEAR: **F**alse **E**vidence **A**ppearing **R**eal!

As I stated before, I have held back so long in sharing my grief that now is the time to show how God worked in my life as He carried me "in HIS strength." So many times, the footprints seen in my mind were those of Jesus carrying me. "The Lord is my strength and my song" (Ex. 15:2 NIV). He sings over me.

I can't help but wonder where my life would have ventured without God. He turned me around, showing His love and care to someone who was no doubt always feeling "not loved." So many times, I heard "You don't belong here," "why are you still around?" "Nobody wants you, can't you get this through your head?" This was the beginning of my fear factor.

I'm getting a little ahead of myself yet these voices still penetrate my heart – a word, a touch, or when I'm feeling down. God does care and I'm forever His very own. Looking back is not easy when you know it's not God's way. Maybe my story can help someone walking in this fearful place.

My first memory is that of a gravesite. I'm 75 years old and this memory is still there and it resonates occasionally. No doubt, the grave was that of my mother, Avey. She died giving birth to my twin sisters, Doris and Iris.

A kind lady gave me a delicate twig of fern at the grave to remember my mother. I cherished that small piece of fern, placing it in a small Bible I was given by someone I didn't even know. I remember looking at this piece of fern and wondering what it had to do with my mother's death. I just didn't understand.

You see, I was just a small two-year old, wondering what was happening to my mother. Children remember tragedies no matter the age. As I said before, memories last a lifetime. I've learned to live with these memories.

Shortly after Mother's death, my brother Robert, baby sisters Doris and Iris, and I were placed in an orphanage in Cedartown, Georgia where we lived for about three years.

In the orphanage, I remember running around in circles as they tried to place a bowl over my curly head so that my long curls could be cut. We all looked the same. Memories come and go as I lived there, but dipping oatmeal at breakfast was my daily chore and standing at the gate on the weekends, waiting for someone to come and pick me up, begging someone on the outside to come in and get me behind the iron gates.

My only security was a little naked rubber doll. We were allowed one toy and this doll was my friend, my feeling of security. Here again is that fear factor creeping in.

Robert stayed in another house, but I cried so much he would come and sleep on the floor by my bed most nights. Robert is three years older than I am. I knew no family except Robert and for most of my early life I didn't know I had family. He was always caring for me. Later in life, for instance, his first assignment being a school patrol leader was taken away when he saw a young boy pulling my long, braided hair over and over. I began to cry and Robert came to my rescue. The principal immediately relieved him of his duties. He was on guard for me always, but not where the pain hurt the deepest. I just couldn't tell him.

For some reason my father wouldn't allow us to be adopted I learned, much later. Never will understand why.

Doris and Iris, still young babies, died in the orphanage. Robert and I were the only family members at Iris's funeral. The other children walked around us after the funeral service and put pennies in our lap to show their hurt for us.

I learned long after mother's death just how hard she worked and how hard her life was. As I understand, she had the twins then returned immediately to the cotton fields. She made her own clothes, mostly out of feed sacks. She died after their births from kidney disease. God took her out of these conditions. She has two of her children with her in heaven. I've only seen a few pictures of her but know she waits for us.

My dad was married five times, one before my mother and three after her. There are twenty-one children involved in all his marriages. Some I know, others I do not. I only have one real brother, Robert, we have the same mother and father. The others are half and step. None know my story.

Soon after my mother's death, my father married his third wife. She had a son from a previous marriage. My father took us from the orphanage and we moved to LaGrange, Georgia to live with them. I was about five years old. Robert and I were scared to death as we moved. Here is the fear factor again.

Rejection and physical abuse came early in my life. Our stepmother didn't like us at all. She and my dad had a child of their own.

I remember a time she chained us to the well as punishment for an accident. We were playing when my half brother fell against the barn door. When he crashed into it, the door flew open and he fell against a rock and started bleeding. It scared us to death. That was punishment enough for us, but not my stepmother. She chained us up like two dogs. Daddy came home from work while we were chained. The next thing I knew we were headed to Macon, Georgia on the back of a motorcycle.

Later, all of us, even my stepmother, half-brother, and her son, moved into a small house on Rock Street. I now know that cousins lived also on this street because when our house burned, they were blamed. I have since learned it was a stove fire.

My daily duty on Rock Street was to carry out what was called a slop jar, or potty, as we had no indoor plumbing. Every morning I had to carry it to the outside toilet to empty the night waste. One particular day as I was doing this chore, I heard shouts of joy, music and firecrackers, and learned the war was over.

My first remembrance of sexual abuse started in this house. I slept in a baby crib and one night I felt someone touching me. Even today, that touch remains. I started to cry but a hand went over my mouth. I saw my own father and was frightened even more, fear to tell—fear not to tell. The next morning when he left for work, I told my stepmother. She put me in a corner immediately and made me drink buttermilk as a punishment for lying. I threw up so much and kept throwing up. When daddy came in from work that afternoon, I was still in the corner with throw-up all over my dress. My stepmother told daddy what happened. He gave me a beating for telling. He told me if I ever told anyone, ever, he would kill me or send me off to jail. I believed him. I was scared to death. I continued living in fear.

Remember that precious piece of fern I had from mother's grave? It was in a safe place I thought, my little Bible. Well, it was in the house on Rock Street when it burned to the ground. I cried for weeks. This piece of fern was all I had to remember my mother's death. I wanted so badly to have her back. That hole remains today. Jesus Christ walks with me daily, helping me fill this hole.

After the fire, Daddy took Robert and me from Rock Street to a boarding house in the Macon Textile Mill Village. He stayed a while at the boarding house, but before long, he was gone. He came and went most of my life. I never knew what happened to our stepmother. She was gone, along with our half-brother and her son.

Still, the abuse continued at Mema's boarding house. I could never tell her. "Fear" was always there controlling me. I had to do what he said or go to jail — so I thought. I've learned in my lifetime that this is how Satan works. Evil tries to steal happiness. To my life he must have thought he was doing a good job.

Mema was good to us, but she never knew. She was good for both of us and assigned us chores. I ironed for the boarders, set tables, things like that; Robert raked yards and took out trash. This was how we paid for our room and board. She didn't openly show love but by taking care of us she did. I learned a lot from Mema. Going to church and school was tops to her. We listened to stories on her radio and I still remember her phone number: 562W. God put her into our lives to give me hope.

Little did I know that this boarding house would be considered my home. We left and came back more times than I can remember. I had been in eight different schools before I was twelve years old. When Dad got mad with a new woman, he came back to the boarding house to visit us, staying a few days. I never knew where he was or when he would show up. Robert and I begged to be left with Mema but he wouldn't let us. We never knew where we would land when we came home from school. We knew we couldn't dare ask any questions.

Mema was with us even into our early teen years. When daddy got upset (mad) with his wife, like

I said before, off we went to Mema's, again and again. Nothing was ever stable.

I first came in contact with the Bible and God through Mema. She made me pray every night. I didn't know how, what for, or why. She always said this was good for me. So I did it. If we didn't go to church, we had to take castor oil and be put to bed.

The Salvation Army supplied our clothes and shoes. I have cried many a tear because I always looked thrown away. Clean, yes, but nothing ever fit just right. Once a month we went to get clothes. My fancy feet show the scars of wearing too big or little shoes, even today. I thank Salvation Army for their good work. They provided clothes for us, extra money for Mema.

When I was at Bellevue Elementary, I was chosen to be a princess. During this time, I found out I had a half-brother who had been looking for us and through Mema, he found us. He was my mother's son from a previous marriage and had been discharged from the Army. He brought me a princess dress, much to my surprise and delight, as the one I had to wear was atrocious.

Daddy didn't like him so he was not allowed to get to know us. He had to stay away until I was much older. He loved us, we just didn't know it. He had been looking for us for years and finally found us.

From Mema's, we moved to another town with a new stepmother. There again we never knew where we would be. The abuse always continued. I hated being alone in any house.

She had four children. Age wise we fit between them: 7, 8 (me), 9, 10, 11 (Robert), 12. Again, that fear was ever present as their mother wasn't very pleased with us. We always had chores. The yard must be swept clean, (brush broom) no grass. We all had work duties every day except Sundays. The house had four rooms; two beds in each room. Working in the fields leaning on the hoe kept me in trouble and to the okra patch I would go or to the rose garden, all the while wearing a dress.

Our Christmas presents were fruit and nuts. Getting a phone and later black and white TV was an exciting time for us. First joy I remember.

One day a box, like a toy box, appeared with a

large lock on it. Couldn't ask daddy questions because he would whip me for asking. Later this stepmother was gone overnight and returned with a baby, my new half-sister. When she returned, the box was opened and it was full of baby clothes. The baby was such a joy to me, I loved her so. To me she was a gift from God because I was allowed to help care for her.

We milked cows, fed hogs, and went to rabbit boxes each morning before school, hunted birds, and picked wild berries for food. I could see chickens under the floor of the house. Poor we were but dad always had the best of cars. We fought over feed sacks for our clothes. Life in this town as usual, he continued the abuse. We had a fruit store. I was made to go with him knowing what was going to happen, always being reminded of jail and no one would believe me. We took baths in a large tub in the backyard where everyone could see because our house had no plumbing inside. We used the outhouse and a Sears & Roebuck catalog served as our tissue.

The girls were always getting their hair done. I begged my stepmother to talk my daddy into letting me get a perm. My thick hair was long and usually I wore braids. Finally, he agreed and off to the School of Hair Design I went, only to realize he would not let them cut my hair. I believe I had the first afro ever. My hair looked horrible. Tears and more tears did not help. I had to go to school looking awful. Washing with Octagon soap finally straightened my hair. All my siblings thought this was so funny. I have thick hair still today.

On rare occasion, if we were "good," our stepmother and daddy took us to an outdoor movie. We usually didn't make it to the movie because we misbehaved or made too much noise for my daddy. We rode in the back of an old truck, holding on for dear life to the cab, hoping not to crash.

One good thing in this town was our school. My brother and I could sing so the school would allow us to sing at special events. Why God gave us our singing voices, I'll never know. I did enjoy singing about God and to Him as I was growing up, even into my adult life. You lose His gifts if you don't use them. My singing voice is gone as I gave up solo singing to sit with my husband at church. God still hears my squeaking voice and knows how much I love praising Him.

As was the norm, I was told we were moving to another town but was not allowed to ask any questions; I was just told "we are moving" and we did.

The first day of school was awful in this new town. The other children laughed at me and told me to go back where I came from. You remember and forgive, but I still know the girl who introduced me to another kind of abuse. Words hurt. This was a defining time in my life. I knew as I was going here and there that painful words were in my life but never came face-to-face with them outside of what I called family.

The house in this town was so much larger than the one before. We still had two regular beds in our room and the boys' room, plus we had indoor plumbing. My stepmother's oldest daughter had her own room. The yards were large and the house was large, which meant more work for us. The garden was small, not like the fields.

Our fun, if you called it fun, on Saturday

afternoons when the others were home was counting cars as they went by. We sat on the bank and watched them pass. We lived close to downtown and the traffic gave us something to do if we weren't working.

Our next-door neighbors had two boys and we learned to kiss using them as boyfriends. The oldest step-sister started this so we all joined in. I was scared to death my dad would catch me. That's what I knew about kissing. Sounds odd now, but that was another fun thing for us.

One day when Robert and I came home from school, Daddy said "get ready we are going to a funeral". Unbeknownst to us we had a brother that died trying to swim across a river on his lunch break. He was 18, but we never knew about him. At the visitation, we went in and looked at him in the casket, then came home, never to mention his name again. He looked just like daddy, found out about him and his life much later in my life. My sister in law found him on line. He was a great guy. I would love to have known him.

At age 14, Dad got me a job. I sold shoes at a

clothing store. I had to go out on the sidewalk and beg people to come into the shop and buy shoes. All the money went to Daddy for my care.

Robert and my step-brother had a paper route. We all worked inside and outside of the house doing something toward our support, "earning our keep" we were told.

One job I really enjoyed was babysitting the preacher's children. Just like my half-sister, I would rock them and sing to them. I was always afraid to go home because I knew what was waiting for me when I got home late. Even with everyone in the house, there was a hall I was made to go to. Still to this day I don't know why someone didn't rescue me from this pain.

My stepsisters, stepbrother, and Robert were always going somewhere. I begged them not to leave me alone. They didn't know the real reason, and I couldn't tell them. If everyone was gone, I knew what would happen. Fear was always with me. One time, I planned to run away, had my clothes on under the covers. Daddy came to my room and for some reason he knew what I was planning. He jerked the covers back, I was fully dressed. His words were that he would kill me or put me in jail. He said no one would believe me anyway and walked out. It scared my sister to death as she was right beside me and knew my plans. Fear, my constant companion, prevented me from leaving, where would I go, what would I do? I couldn't tell my brother Robert, I was in fear for him and thought Dad would kill him. I believe to this day that my stepmother knew what was happening to me and did nothing. I went to school, worked, did chores, and helped with the baby as she was growing up, hoping nothing would happen to her.

In her own way, our stepmother always let me know I was a "step" child. I never felt I belonged. I was never good enough, no matter how I tried. For some reason Robert and I stood out to people, which she didn't like. I was never allowed to wear normal clothes. Even her mother, Mammy, felt for us saying she prayed for us to be grown soon. I had to wear a dress while my new stepsisters and half-sister could wear anything. They wore pants, jeans, shorts, whatever they wanted, I could not, I had to be different. I hid my life from my classmates, even

Mary Ann and Nancy, fearful they would tell someone and off to jail I would go. Fear eats at a teenager. Classmates never knew. I had in my head "who would believe a teenager anyway." I was the great pretender.

At school, the teachers would let me sit with their class as a substitute teacher if they had an appointment. Future Homemakers of America (FHA) allowed me to learn so much about the other side of life I never knew. This organization was a great lift in my life. I am so grateful for my education.

Again, I tried hard to fit in somewhere. School took me away from what was at home. I was good at wearing a mask and hiding … always hiding.

As far as any activities, that was a joke. All the others could go to the movies, date, even go skating, the favorite Friday night fun. One night, and I mean ONE night, I was allowed to go skating. I wore jeans hidden under my dress. Daddy finally agreed to let me go. When I got to the skating rink, I took the dress off and wore jeans like everyone else. Would you believe my daddy showed up checking on me, not the others, and I wasn't allowed to go again. The ugly, thick belt waited for me when I got home. My life was a prison; church was my only outlet. I was allowed to go to church where I thought I could be me, even though I still wore the mask there. Thank you, Jesus, for the church where I knew You were.

Like I said before, the only place I could go alone was to church, where I gave my life to Jesus. Learning about Him and memorizing His word has sustained me through many trying times. He became my Father, Mother, Brother, Sister, my All. Later I learned Psalm 34:18, which says, "The Lord is close to the brokenhearted and saves those who are crushed in spirit." But at the time, I didn't fully understand just how much He loved me. Today, I claim Psalm 23 as my own. I walked in the valley of the shadow of death most of my early life. I prayed, asking God where He was and in the corner of my eye I saw someone saying, "I'm here. I am your Father, Mother, Sister and Brother. I'll never leave or forsake you." At that time, I didn't know this was also in the Bible. When I found these words in Deuteronomy 6 (NIV), my heart melted. I cried and cried.

It took me twenty-five plus years, and after my father's death, before I told a soul of the sexual abuse. I just knew my dad would kill me or send me away to what he called the chain gang. He repeated this threat many more times during my childhood through my teenage years. He beat me with a leather belt or a large switch; I was his whipping boy. The more I cried the more he beat me, no matter what I did wrong. He dared me to cry. His switchings cut so deep that my legs bled. He was a violent person. I couldn't do anything right. He didn't like me at all. I hated to see him coming as he rarely stayed at home. If he was home, the fear swelled up in me, almost bursting my heart.

I had a battle with self-esteem even into adult life. Abuse, no matter whether it is verbal, sexual, or physical, can rob you of your life if you let it. It almost took my life. It has taken a lifetime for me to finally write this book. For some reason, abuse, especially sexual, makes you feel it's your fault. You always feel as if you've done something wrong and you're afraid to tell anyone – I'm to blame and not knowing what to do about these feelings – I faulted myself for not speaking up. Speak up, my friends, don't let the destroyer take your life.

Even today, fear tries to raise its ugly head, especially when I am by myself in a crowd and don't know anyone. It's a lonely feeling.

My brother Robert left me when I was about 14, joining the Navy to get away. He said he was tired of taking care of me; he always took care of me. He ran away just as I wished I could. I was more alone than ever. He never knew my real pain but tried to care for me as best he could. Dad was mean to him, too. Daddy was not allowed to touch my step-siblings, instructions from their mother, so Robert and I got the brunt of his anger.

At fifteen and a half I ran from the frying pan into the fire. I got married. I had no idea what marriage was all about. I had to get out. I ran, not realizing I would hurt others down the road.

Hard to believe, but the main reason I got married was because my stepmother told my dad I sat on a boy's lap. He beat me so badly that night the belt buckle imprint stayed on my side for a month. The scar is still on me today. I had bruises all over my body. He made me go to school or said he would send me to jail. I looked awful. My teacher asked how I got the bruises but I couldn't say a word. My stepmother watched and did nothing, again and again. Everyone in the family feared him. She may have, too. Fear may have held her bondage, too. She never said a word about his actions.

As I think back now, daddy had to sign for me to get married. He must have found a new wife as he left this stepmother shortly thereafter, moving to another state. I married the guy whose lap I sat on.

That first night of marriage, I washed my feet, staying in the bathroom all night. My new husband didn't seem to mind but I knew what he was waiting for. No feelings just lying there like I had most of my abusive life. Alone with him was fear all the time.

My first marriage was like being with daddy; I felt sex was the only reason. Fear still lived with me when we were alone. I had no idea what to do. I felt that jail was always waiting for me. Love just wasn't in the picture. I married the family, not my husband. My past was always in the middle of my marriage and fear never left. Terror was always present.

We lived with his parents at first while I was in school, which gave me someone to talk to. One of his sisters taught me how to dress, walk, and act. She stays deep in my heart today for her goodness, kindness, and love. But I held a constant fear she would find out about me. She asked many, many times if there was something wrong. As I look back God had all of them in place, I just had allowed evil to conquer my life. Loving Jesus I did, but evil seemed to take over my life no matter how I tried to let go. There were wonderful loving people, I just couldn't for the life of me let them in. My shield was too thick. I always anticipated danger.

I married into a caring family who took me in and loved me as I had never been loved. However, I was always on guard, though, and didn't trust them for many years. Eventually, I saw that they loved me for no reason. They just loved. I didn't understand this love at all. This was so strange, and I really couldn't believe it. I always had dreams of a family, I pretended I belonged to them. Mind you, I never forgot I was an in-law, but his family took good care of me and I will never forget them.

My pain of feeling dirty and at fault grew and I couldn't understand, even as the family tried to make me feel part of them. So much damage had been done it was hard to feel good about myself.

He wasn't a violent man around others until it came to sexual relationship, I did the same with him as I did with my daddy. Just laid there, which made him so mad. Words hurt sometimes as bad as sexual abuse – maybe worse. Always spoken in the bedroom, never around other family members. He worked shift work and many weeks we didn't even see each other. I was in school, he worked. I can't fault him as the struggle was me, not him.

Once in this early marriage, maybe 17 years old, I tried to commit suicide by cutting my wrist, I wanted out. My mother-in-law got so mad, the only time I ever saw her really mad. She told me I was God's child and what I did was against Him. I still see the scene in my mind to this day. I disappointed her and hurt a person who loved me. She continued her love and never spoke of this again. I know now she was trying to help me, not hurt me, but I always was on guard. They were real; they just loved someone who feared accepting their love.

I graduated from high school, the only person in school married. I still pretended I was like everyone else. I wore my mask so well no one ever suspected my secret. No one ever knew my pain. I slipped around and wore my friend's clothes, changing at school, hoping to feel and look like everyone else. Very close friends knew about the beatings but not about the sexual abuse.

Questions for Reflection

1) Have you ever felt unwanted or unloved?

2) Did fear fit into these feelings?

3) Where was God in your feelings of fear?

4) Did you feel His presence as you walked through these feelings? How?

5) Where are you today in reference to these fears in your past? Are you still wrestling with them?

6) Do words hurt you? If so, how deep?

7) Were you ever afraid to go home? If so, why?

8) What did you do instead?

FORGIVENESS

"Bear with each other and forgive one another if any of you has a grievance against someone. Forgive as the Lord forgave you." Col. 3:15 NIV

"Let all bitterness, wrath, anger, clamor, and evil speaking be put away from you, with all malice." Eph. 4:31 NKJV

If you are still haunted by sin and bitterness and its actions, knowing God has forgiven you, think of it the way David did: out of sight, out of mind, never to be seen or thought of again. Hard as it seems, it can be done.

"In these days of guilt complexes, perhaps the most glorious word in the English language is 'forgiveness'." Billy Graham

Hate and bitterness controlled my life deep inside. After graduation from high school, I got on a Greyhound bus and went to Hot Springs, Arkansas, where my daddy lived with a new stepmother, to tell my daddy how much I hated him. He was sitting at the kitchen table with a new half-brother. Later a half-sister was born. I never knew them while they were small, but finally found them after much research, and love them dearly. I did just that, got back on the bus with great satisfaction. Growing with God, I learned that I had to forgive him, which was my desire. I did forgive him. One day, I called him to ask forgiveness for my bitterness, but only reached his voice mail, so I left a message. A couple of hours later, I learned he'd died that very day. I never spoke to him.

Forgiveness, I learned, was not between me and my dad but between me and God. I had to put on His righteousness (cover my heart) to obey and do His will. I learned forgiveness had to come from my forgiving before it comes to me, because I was shackled in my pain. I forgave my father and this set me free. WOW, what a feeling.

Don't wait like I did, bitterness grows and

destroys you, not the person who harmed you. Forgiveness sets you free. Ephesians 4:31 says "get rid of all bitterness, forgive each other as Christ forgave you." I wanted to be rid of the fear and bitterness I had built up against my father for so many years.

I have learned over the years that unforgiveness can be stuffed inside and kept bottled up where it turns to hatred or retaliation against the person. I took vengeance in my own hands, trying to repay the wrong daddy did to me. God had a different plan for me.

By graduation, I was pregnant with the joy of my life, my son Joel. He brought me joy but also grave responsibility. I thought I knew about babies, but soon realized how little I knew. I knew nothing about caring for a baby. Growing up with both physical and sexual abuse, I cry when I think of the physical abuse I did to my son. I was too physically strict, too hard, but I did give him my love. He was my heart, yet I took it out on him. I finally realized just how hard I was when he was about ten. I hit him hard and he asked was I trying to kill him. I asked him for forgiveness and received it. Forgiving myself, loving myself was my challenge.

In my first marriage of seven years, I had a miscarriage and lost a child during a serious bout of the flu. Packed in ice, the doctors thought I was dying.

I experienced going through a tunnel and seeing light coming out. I heard a strong voice, "Estelle, are you ready?" I said "No." Can you believe I said "No" to God? I explained that I had to care for my son. Immediately, I came to. Everyone around me was crying. God was with me all the time, I just didn't call on Him. He hears your cries, bottles your tears, I learned this the hard way.

I immediately went to my pastor who said I had an out of the body experience.

"He" knows my name. He knows your name.

Even with this experience, it wasn't enough to save our marriage. My feelings were not there. Because of my past, we fussed and fought so much that finally I filed for a divorce, moved out with Joel.

My car was packed with no place to go. No known family except my brother who had troubles of his own. I went to my work. At work, a lady everyone thought was not so nice, turned out to be my "angel" in disguise. She let us use a basement apartment to live in. Basement, means basement, the grass almost covered the windows. When I looked out, grass was there. We had a bed, kitchen table, four chairs, refrigerator, and stove.

The vehicle I drove each day to work had the motor in the back of the car. I carried an extra fan belt with my tools and many times I had to stop to change the fan belt on my car. For some reason God provided me with this ability. I was dressed for work on the side of the road and no one paid any attention. We see people in need all the time but our 24 hours seem to be more important. Everyone is in such a hurry, always rushing, not seeing those in need. I know now I should always have lived by faith, not by sight as 2 Corinthians 5:7 says, but this was one hard thing for me to do. God supplies our needs even when we don't ask for them.

Shortly after we moved into the basement apartment, my car was repossessed (no money) so we walked everywhere, to work, to the nursery, to the laundromat and grocery store. I had no transportation. My salary was very small. It was hard. I had no one. It seemed all my life I had no one, no one to call on. I just didn't understand. Why me? No matter what God had in mind for me, I still wondered, why? Life was so hard but His strength kept me going. Looking back, I can see just how much HE carried me. We may not feel it, think it or know it, but He is always with us. HE is family.

As I said, I did graduate and immediately got a job at a local bank. That in itself kept me busy but every man I saw I thought they were just like in my past. Good people most likely, but a shield covered me for protection from everyone, always on guard.

My second job was with an insurance company. I loved the sweet co-worker but one of the owners liked me, I thought a little too much, and every day I was again living in fear. Nothing happened but I knew by his actions what he was thinking, my guard was up. At the office lunch, he put a $100.00 bill under a drink and dared me to drink it. I did not. He had different ideas I just know. One thing I did learn from my daddy was always be in control never let anyone control you. Daddy controlled me for many, many years, most of my life but now I can say that freedom feels so much better. Wherever my Savior leads me, I want to follow: I want my Lord to control my life. Like I said before, freedom feels so much better.

God was providing for us, where the food came from, I don't know. I just didn't see it at the time. Looking back, you can see God's presence. It's hard sometimes while you are in the storm. He does some of HIS best work in the middle of a storm.

Joel and I moved into a basement, trying to make a living for us. Little did I know this was the best thing I ever did. I met Robert, my future husband – the love of my life.

Still, I took my frustrations out on Joel. He was my heart, yet he experienced my grief and my anger. I'll never forget, yet I am forgiven by my Lord and him. Those memories are still with me. The pain I caused him is always with me, it just doesn't go away. We went through hell together. I was always fighting to survive. God has plans for us, HE really does. His hands hold us. Only if we will let HIM. HE will not push HIS way into our lives but is always waiting for us to call HIM.

Questions for Reflection

1) When have you asked someone to forgive you. How did it effect your relationship? Did it change?

2) How can you break the cycle of unforgiveness, bitterness, wrath and anger?

3) Have you accepted God's gift of forgiveness? If not, what actions need to be taken?

4) Have you found it difficult to forgive yourself for something you have done or failed to do?

5) How many times must you forgive someone who has caused you pain?

FAMILY/FRIENDS

"Because you are his sons, God sent the Spirit of his Son into our hearts, the Spirit who calls out, *"Abba*, Father." So you are no longer a slave, but God's child; and since you are his child, God has made you also an heir." Gal. 4:6-7 NIV

"If anyone does not provide for his relatives, especially for immediate family, he has denied the faith and is worse than an unbeliever." 1 Timothy 5:8 NIV

Four Basic Needs:

    1) Belonging

    2) Approval

    3) Worth

    4) LOVE

During this time, my newly found cousin invited me to go with her to the Varsity. This was, unbeknownst to me, the place to go and meet guys or girls to date. I hated men but after much insistence I went. Remember I had a child, no money, no anything. Psalm 23 carried me through — He will NEVER leave you or forsake you. NEVER.

My cousin had broken off with this guy, but they remained friends. When I met him, he thought he was God's gift to women. (Remember, my opinion, hating men). He was nice looking and built with big muscles, like his shirt was too small. We said few words, so I left and came home, not thinking much about us meeting.

The next day, he called me to ask us to the movies. I said no, as I had no intention of dating him. He called the next day, I said no. I said I didn't know him well enough. The next week he called again. I really didn't want to know him, so I said no, I didn't know him well enough. His response was, "My number is 956-3011. I want to date you, get to know you and your son. Call me if you change your mind." After much encouragement from my friends, I called him the next week and we began dating. Joel, around four years old at the time, was a little standoffish, but Robert soon won him over with lots of laughter and jokes.

That was over 50 years ago. I can't believe I still remember Robert's phone number today.

One lunch date with him the whole building opened their windows and clapped as we went to lunch. They thought (the people in the building) that I would never meet a man that I could get close to, much less love. I laugh seeing this sight in my mind today. They all waved and clapped as we walked away.

A co-worker asked that Joel and I move in with her to help with finances, which we did. She had two children who accepted us so kindly. She helped me get out from the basement into a real home. Remember, the basement had only a bed, table with four chairs, old stove and refrigerator. Living with her was like heaven.

I was dating Robert steady and every now and then we went to a place called Lake Henry to dance. Remember all this was pretty new to me. The only outside world around me was in school and church. I learned dancing in school. Poor Robert took the brunt of my two left feet.

Robert was in school and worked various jobs and studied. We saw him when he was taking a break. He introduced me to drinking, dancing and having fun. So different for me, yet down deep I was scared to death. Even kissing brought fear. He never said anything but I always wondered if he knew I had been abused. Thoughts can destroy you, all this was my thinking in my head. Quiet, I mean quiet he was, but caring and gentle. The word "gentleman" describes him so well.

Robert was like a knight in shining armor. He made us feel like we were special, part of something good. He would spend weekends with my son at his parents' home. They really had a good time together. We had fun together. Nothing was required of me. He treated me special.

Robert was a Christian. His parents loved the Lord. They embraced us with love and kindness. Again, I was always on guard. I trusted no one, always waiting for the worst to happen. They took us in like we were their very own.

Before Robert asked me to marry him, he had a long talk with his mother who told him to care for my son like he was his very own. This he did and adopted him years later at the insistence of Joel. Joy, joy, joy came into my life. We married, no honeymoon, moved into a $50.00 per month duplex, went to work and school the next morning. This was our life for many years. How we made it, I'll never know. However, our Lord knew this I know now.

We dated a year before we married. I wanted my son and Robert to bond. Plus, the fear factor still stayed deep in my heart. I couldn't believe he really loved me. I kept wondering, Why? Was I good enough? I was damaged. I was abused. I carried all this into our marriage. I kept this secret way down deep. I surely couldn't tell Robert. Loving Robert sexually was hard. I felt so ashamed. This took a long process. Sometime a word or touch brings back awful memories even today. Again, that's how evil works.

I'm thankful for a great doctor who helped me see that sex could be good. In marriage, it is a special gift. His wise counsel probably saved my marriage.

You see, Robert never knew. I hid my fears. I feared the day he would find out. I had to tell him many, many years later. I had to give my testimony in order to go on the church's mission trip. Little did I know HE was planning my own mission trip to help others. No one in my family knew. I had to tell all of them. This was one of the hardest things I had ever done. All the pain tried to surface again, but God took control.

Our daughter was born six weeks before Robert's college graduation. She was a beauty and Joel's delight.

After college, Robert went on to law school. I told the world of Robert's passing the bar before he got the chance. He did get in one call. That's how excited I was at the time. He had worked so hard for this achievement. He worked evening and midnight shifts and attended school during the day while I worked.

We learned from trials that came and went in our home, but He has protected us always walking by our side. His word has sustained our family.

One night, we had two children. Then Robert's sister and brother-in-law died, and through a Will, the next night we had three children, welcoming a heart-broken ten-year old little girl into our family. We knew the right thing to do was to help our niece, a sweet, frightened child, by showing love and support. Through much heartache and pain from other family members, she continued to live with us and stands firm for our Lord Jesus. Her walk through early life was not easy but she shines for Him today. He covered her then as He does now. She is such a blessing.

Our Lord has given me a new heart in my walk and I praise Him for this. We all know Him as our Savior to this day. Halleujah – what a Savior we serve.

In the last years of college, we met friends who stayed with us through graduation from law school until this day. We have so many supporters, sent by God Himself.

These friends loved us like brothers/ sisters, like Scripture says, and they remain so dear to us to this day. I could cook hamburger meat for dinner in one hundred different ways. One Thanksgiving the three couples had turkey with the complete insides (neatly in the plastic package). We cleaned each others' homes and would give items away that were not used in the past year. I confess I do not do this today – confession is good for the soul.

By this time, I had moved on to working at a military facility, making a little more money for our family.

We met another couple, during my pregnancy, when our son Joel had to have a tonsillectomy. In the hospital, pregnant with daughter, I met this beautiful sexy lady wearing go-go boots.

Her son, Mark, was also having surgery. She was the only woman I ever allowed Robert to spend the night with.

From that time on we usually went to their home and played cards – socialized. Poor as we were they provided years of fun and laughter.

To this day, God has allowed a lasting friendship – young at heart we remain although the body tries to tell us different. Psalm 90:24(b) in the

NIV describes our friendship, "but real friends stick closer than a brother."

We went to church but 'going' and 'doing' are two different things. Our neighbors across the street kept inviting us to come to their church. We did and have been faithful ever since. God used them to bring us back to Him. He uses His saints every day.

Our children are almost seven years apart. My thinking was God knew I could care for one child at a time, especially in their most crucial years called teenage years.

Our son had to deal with my divorce, a new dad, new friends, and school, plus all the internal changes. Growing up was hard on him at first, but getting serious about our relationship with Jesus allowed him to see the changes in us. Children are caught more than taught. This we learned the hard way.

My guilt lead to so much heartache on my family. Our Lord took over our lives. God does hear our cries and does pay attention to our prayers. He was my strength then as He is now. I know from experience. He never leaves us for one second. But during this time, we would put Him on the shelf and call on Him when we were in a stressful situation, but no more.

On the other hand, our daughter spent her life growing up, trying to be the best she could be. Our struggles caused her to try to be that perfect daughter. I thank my Lord that He was her support. She could and would lean on Him always. What strength she has.

Walking with a sweet, sweet couple through the deep valley of divorce has given me a lasting, growing friendship. God works in mysterious ways – He really does.

My beautiful friend lost her husband, Tommy, and her sister, but through her own illness, her words of encouragement to me always calms my nerves.

Three dear friends and I call ourselves the "Twisted Sisters." They have listened to my cries, heard my struggles, and given me Godly wisdom. Love them dearly. Couldn't do without them. They are my support. They have their own struggles but always have time for me.

He allowed me to meet this beautiful woman whose husband suffered a horrible wreck. I have watched her love for God and His strength carry her through this tragedy. She never flinched, just submitted to God and did what she had to do to care for him. She cares for her husband today. God walked and still walks with her. I am honored to be called her friend. What strength.

Cancer has tried three times to steal joy from this beautiful, energetic sweet friend who wants to help and does help everyone she meets, greeting everyone with the most beautiful smile. She is in remission now but pushes on every minute of the day. What joy just being around her.

My hero is my small red headed friend who walks daily with God. I call her my partner in crime. Watching her handle her husband's cancer has been unbelievable. He has gone over two years with three kinds of cancer. Again, what strength, what patience.

Our friends in St. Simons keep their doors always open to us. What joy and wisdom they bring. They have walked beside us through many trying times.

Watching LH care for her husband of over 30 years after he was diagnosed with a crippling disease early in their marriage is a memory I'll never forget. Gentle, kind, loving, caring – these words define her well and serve as a lesson to us all. Through all the pain they endured and her husband's eventual death, she maintained her joy and her faith. She is now remarried to one of their college friends and she is always willing to help others.

My dear sister-in-love, MA has always been right there in any area of my life. I call, she is there. Beautiful inside and out, always helping others.

Prayer warriors P & Z always near and dear. A phone call is all that is required. Prayer warriors they are, always having a heart for others.

The person doing my typing and corrections before this manuscript goes to my editor has walked through trials, tears, and pain with me over twenty-five years! I thank her for her love of our Lord. Her struggles are hidden deep, but she carries on depending on Him, her Savior.

There are so many others God has placed in my life as support. I could go on naming them. Praise

God they all depend on HIM completely. To God be the Glory!

Questions for Reflection

1) On a scale of 1 to 10, how hard is it for you to forgive others?

2) Are you a forgiving person? Why or Why not?

3) For what invisible pain do you need to ask God's forgiveness?

4) Do you believe not forgiving yourself or others affects you today? If so, how?

FREEDOM

"These things I have spoken to you, that My joy may remain in you and that your joy may be full. This is My Commandment that you love 'One another as I have loved you." John 15:11-12 NKJV

"Let all those rejoice who put their trust in you; let them ever shout for joy; let them ever shout for joy because you defend them; Let those also who love Your name be joyful in you. For You, 0 Lord, will bless the righteous; with favor You will surround him as with a shield." Ps. 5:11-12 NKJV

"Do not conform to the pattern of this world." Romans 12:2 NIV

Refuse to let anyone put a label on you. Only God and God alone created you.

If you are walking through any of this, talk to someone. Please seek counsel. You can be set free. Don't let the chains of the past keep you down. Don't let your past define you. He has great peace for all of us. Claim it. Remember the victories God has given you in the past, and accept who He has made you to be.

We tend to place labels on ourselves, good or bad. We allow parents, teachers, a job, a coach to identify who we are. These labels can shape our future. Only our Heavenly Father who molded us, purchased us, sent His Son who paid for our sins on the cross can label us. We are His and His alone. I labeled myself for many, many years as belonging to no one. I'm His and He is mine – so Free.

God sent Robert to us, no doubt. It took some time to fully see this, but looking back, I know God delivered him to us using my cousin. He put her in my path. God works in mysterious ways. In our marriage, we have had our ups and downs but God has given me a wonderful husband, children, grandchildren, and a great grandchild.

God is always with us. We may wander away

but He said, "I'll never leave you or forsake you." No matter where you are, He is waiting for you to ask Him in. His strength changed my life. He can change yours. It took a while but I finally gave Him my all. He gave me freedom.

In His strength, through the Holy Spirit, He used my life to help a little girl whose mother and father died fourteen months apart. I could never have cared for her the way I did had I not had the experiences in my life. He used something so bad to help a little girl and she never knew my past. I believe now He was molding me to help someone else. She lived in fear too, fear of losing parents fear of living with us. God placed her with us to give her support. My prayer today is that she knows she was loved as she was growing up.

Hearing my story, you'd think I knew better, but our drinking socially, wanting to fit in, contributed to our son's alcoholism. We contributed to his pain. This was hard to admit. Sometimes the consequences of our actions are seen through our children. Thank you Jesus, he sought treatment and twenty years later continues doing great. God sent him a wonderful wife. Her support helped him walk through this trial. God has used his experience many times to give support to others and continues to do so. Only in His strength did we get through this valley. He also uses our struggle to help others. Joel has been set free.

Trials come and go in one's life. Our daughter was involved in an auto accident where a young guy wanted to die and take someone with him. He was drunk. He almost took her. To see her today, you'd never believe what I'm saying. Her face is held together with wires and metal. Again, this was alcohol. We shared with this young man, forgave him, and God has used this accident so many times to comfort someone else. God allows us to feel others' pain, to grieve with them.

Our church family (my family), has provided support each and every time. Like I said before, God has provided many people to walk me through my life. I have named a few and I am so, so grateful. Without them I wonder where I would have been. If you are not in a church family, I pray you will find one that fits you. Church is important to God and I pray it will be important to you too.

God supplies all your needs in Christ Jesus. When our house burned, we moved into the church house and immediately our church family went to work making us comfortable. We lacked nothing.

Later, He even sent a lady, another angel, to set up and decorate a rented house. To this day none of us, not even our children, remember her name. No matter what you are going through, He'll never leave you or forsake you.

We knew God had plans for us when we purchased a house close to our church home. I never thought of living in this area, never. It's amazing to see His work. He had work for us to do. He allowed us to counsel with many hurting people plus give support to missionaries. He always has a plan for us. Sometimes we rush ahead of Him and we get into trouble. I've been good at going ahead of God most of my life.

He sold our house, our work was finished there. He provided us a home here, near our new church. Our home is His home. He owns it all, we are only here for a while. Heaven waits for us.

I thank God constantly for my life. I'm not bitter, I'm BETTER, but only with His loving strength. Again, it took almost half my life to really say this. My fear is gone, I've been set free. I'm FREE you can be too. Just give it ALL to HIM. Ps. 34:4-19; Ps. 40:1-3 NIV.

You can let your past keep you down or let God use your past to help others. Don't wait as long as I did.

Looking back, I have spent most of my life trying to belong to someone's family with little results. Being married to Robert who had six sisters was my last try. I hated all family occasions because I felt I didn't fit. I couldn't do enough. I tried too hard. I even tried to fit in my brother's wife's family, even asked to be one of them … what was I thinking?

The feelings of not belonging, of being rejected in the past, don't tell who I am today. Don't let the past have the final say in your life either. I can't say this enough.

With Jesus, I am safe forever. I'm forever His, accepted as His child. I'm forever, completely loved. The 'Guide of Life,' the book or Proverbs, showed me God's way. Turn to Him. He is waiting.

There in front of me was my wonderful family: husband, son, daughter, niece and her husband, grandchildren and a great grandchild. That should have been enough but I still felt left out of the real family living. God has forgiven these feelings and I am FREE. I know I am sharing with someone who has or is going through these same feelings but I say to them to look around you — God has not left you out of anything. Fear of rejection causes that feeling. Forgiveness and family bring you right back to Him: FREEDOM.

In my thinking, freedom in life is like the olive tree and the olive. We need both the winds of hardship and the gentle winds of relief to sweep across our lives if we are to be truly fruitful and to go forward doing God's work.

Olives are bitter and must be washed, pressed down, and soaked, over and over again, to produce the oil. This is us, this is me. This kind of hardship process took my bitterness and hatred out of my heart. Second Corinthians 4:8-9 says we may be "hard pressed on every side, but not crushed … struck down, but not destroyed" (NIV).

God does provide support. Look around you, look up, and see Him in action.

Little did I know He would use my life to help someone else. We get caught up in others' sins but God takes that hurt and sadness and uses it to help someone else. Robert and I share our lives as God leads us. We try to help in some small way to give support. Our only desire is to bring the hurting, sad, and lonely to meet our Lord. So if I'm hugging you, know it's an extension of God's love saying to you, "You are special." He loves you and so do I.

Questions for Reflection

1) Do you consider yourself free from your past?

2) When did God take something bad in your life and make it good?

3) Do you use your freedom to help others or yourself? How? Why?

4) Everyone has a free will. How are you exercising your free will since you have been set free?

5) Since you feel free, what are you doing for God in His freedom?

6) How will you change your life since you will give an account of everything you do in your new life of freedom?

A List of Withouts

Without trials, there can be no maturity.

Without clouds, there can be no silver lining.

Without clouds, there can be no appreciation of sunshine.

Without rain, there can be no rainbow.

Without rain, there can be no vegetation.

Without the stress of the storm, we cannot realize the worth of an anchor.

Without darkness, there can be no rest.

Without darkness, we cannot see the stars.

Without night, there can be no sunrise.

Without threshing, we cannot use the wheat.

Without injury and irritation, the oyster will not produce a pearl.

Without a hammer and chisel, the stone cannot become a statue, a work of art, a masterpiece.

Without crushing the flowers, there can be no perfume.

Without trials, we cannot be like Jesus.

Anonymous

About the Author

Estelle "Essie" H. Herndon, is a Christ Follower, wife, mother, grandmother, great-grandmother and prayer warrior. She has worked alongside her husband, Robert, as his paralegal for over forty-seven years.

Essie is active in her church. She teaches with her husband in Bible studies and leading small groups, helping with Women's Ministries and Grief Ministries, from youth to young married adults.

She is also active in her community, having served on various boards over the years.

Her family and friends are her hobbies. She and husband Robert enjoy traveling which has included Georgia football games. She and brother Robert meet almost daily for breakfast.

She truly tries to please God in her daily activities, always remembering where she has been in her past and how God has worked in her life for His Honor. She lives in Georgia.

Loving life. Free in HIS strength!

Thank you
for reading our books.

Look for other books
published by

www.TMPbooks.com

Made in the USA
Columbia, SC
12 October 2022

69343749R00048